Diet recommendations for acute gastritis

Please check these recommendations always with a nutrition consultant, therapist, doctor or dietician. The recipes and the list of ingredients are supporting the conventional medical therapy.
The calorie disclosures of fresh ingredients (fruit and vegetables) vary according to quality and time of harvest. The contents were checked by a dietician and a nutrition consultant for the Traditional Chinese Medicine (TCM).

AF199931

Author:
©2017 Josef Miligui
www.ebns.at

Source:
The lists are created from the EBNS database for nutritional counseling. The database is used by dietitians, therapists and doctors for advising the patient / client.

Literature:
The specialist literature and the training documents of the German and Austrian dietary and traditional Chinese medicine serve as a knowledge base. We have used the documents as a basis of knowledge, adapted it to our experience and completed them.
http://di-book.com

Title Photo:
©2008 Erika Weixlbaumer

Production and publishing:
BoD – Books on Demand, Norderstedt
ISBN 9783746043241

Diet recommendations for DIETETICS - Gastrointestinal tract - Stomach and duodenal intestine - Acute gastritis

1 Treatment strategy

Relax the stomach.
Fennel tea, peppermint tea and chamomile tea (not sweet, neither with

sugar nor with honey) is ideal.
Avoid food which causes pain.
A glass of milk or dairy products such as yogurt or apple sauce are ideally suited as intermediate meals.
Make sure that the stomach is never completely empty.
Mucus soup, rusks, dry pastry.
Afterwards 1-2 days light weight.

2 Avoid

Fats, sour food, alcohol, caffeine.

3 Breakfast

	kkal. per serving
Apple sauce with raisins	73
Barley and vegetable soup	281
Barley soup	265
Buddhist reissue soup	279
Carrot and rice gruel soup	101
Carrots with potato foam	316
Compote from apples	67
Fennel-Rice Soup	155
Kohlrabi in chervil sauce with potatoes	187
Millet mash with steamed pears	235
Noodle soup	236
Pear compote	100
Polenta with peach	197
Purėed banana	144
Quinoa with peach	247
Rice congee with carrots and fennel	131
Rice congee with honey pear and black sesame	158
Rice dulse soup	190
Rice porridge with shrubs (seeds) Yi Yi Ren	211
Rice with parsnips	206
Roasted millet with Celery sticks	400
Rosemary Potatoes	188
Semolina porridge with banana	307
Spring vegetables	63
Tea from anise	2
Tea from fennel	0
Tea Green tea	2
Tea stomach tea	3
Tender fennel vegetables	70

4 Snack

Apple sauce with raisins 73
Banana porridge 235
Carrots with potato foam 316
Millet mash with steamed pears 235
Spring vegetables 63

5 Lunch

Apple sauce with raisins 73
Barley and vegetable soup 281
Barley soup 265
Basmati rice + Zucchini tofu dish 145
Buddhist reissue soup 279
Carrot and rice gruel soup 101
Carrots with potato foam 316
Chicken soup with egg yolk and parsley 117
Compote from apples 67
Fennel-Rice Soup 155
Kohlrabi in chervil sauce with potatoes 187
Noodle soup 236
Pear compote 100
Polenta with peach 197
Puréed banana 144
Rice congee with carrots and fennel 131
Rice congee with honey pear and black sesame 158
Rice dulse soup 190
Rice porridge with shrubs (seeds) Yi Yi Ren 211
Rice with parsnips 206
Roasted millet with Celery sticks 400
Rosemary Potatoes 188
Semolina porridge with banana 307
Spring vegetables 63
Tea from anise 2
Tea from fennel 0
Tea Green tea 2
Tea stomach tea 3
Tender fennel vegetables 70

6 Afternoon

Apple sauce with raisins 73
Carrots with potato foam 316

7 Dinner

8 Any time

9 Recipes

(recommendable) = You can use more.
(little) = You should use less than specified or omit.

9.1 Apple sauce with raisins

Stops diarrhea, promotes digestion, appetizing, relieves diarrhea, activates carbohydrate metabolism.
Cooking time approx. 25 min
Calories p. portion: 74
10 portions
Allergens: O

Quantity of ingredients
Apple (sweet) 2,2 lbs / 1000g. (little)
Water 1/2 cup / 100g. (yes)
Raisins 1/8 lbs - 2oz / 50g. (little)

Cooking instructions:
Wash, peel and quarter the apples and remove the core. Put the apples with the water in a pot. Wash the raisins with hot water and add them. Cook at low heat for about 10 minutes, then allow to cool. For children up to 10 months, mash in the blender finely. For the larger ones, crush with the potato steamer. Fill and seal in a freezer or empty yoghurt jug. Close the yoghurt jug. Freeze in the shock freezer.
If necessary, thaw at room temperature for about 6 hours. (Lasting about 4 months).
The fruit mousse is intended as dessert or intermediate meal. It has an anti-digestive effect. In case of diarrhea give better banana.

9.2 Banana porridge

Regulates gastrointestinal function. Protects the digestive system. Detoxifying, affects anorexia, good to fight flatulence, inflammatory bowel disease.
Cooking time approx. 10 Min
Calories p. portion: 235
1 portions
Allergens: AG

Quantity of ingredients
Water 1/2 cup / 125g. (yes)
Wheat flakes 1/2 oz / 20g. (yes)
Banana 1/4 lbs - 4oz / 100g. (recommended)
Butter organic 1 table spoon / 10g. (yes)

Cooking instructions:
Mix the water with the flakes in a small pan. Bring to boil by low heat, cook for 1-2 minutes and then remove from the cooking area. Cut the banana in pieces into the pot, add the butter and puree with a blender. Fill the banana porridge into a plate (feed the baby with the spoon). (The afternoon porridge is basically cooked only with water, so it is all the more important not to forget to add fat, otherwise your baby is hungry long before the next meal.)
Instead of butter, you can also take corn oil - especially when the porridge is not so hot, the oil is distributed more easily.
If you use buckwheat, millet, corn or rice flakes instead of wheat flakes, the mash is gluten-free.

9.3 Barley and vegetable soup

Supports urination, detoxifying, promotes spleen and liver, reduces blood pressure, strengthens immune system, prevents cancer, reduces radiation damage, promotes digestion, helps to digest fat, harmonizes metabolism.
Cooking time approx. 2 hours
Calories p. portion: 281
3 portions
Allergens: AGL

Quantity of ingredients
Barley 1 cup / 120g. (yes)
Shiitake, dried 1/8 oz / 4g. ()
Onion (shallot) 1 piece / 20g. ()
Cumin (Caraway seed) 1 knife tip / 0,5g. (yes)
Sunflower oil 1 table spoon / 10g. (little)
Water 1 cup / 250g. (yes)
Celery sticks 2 branches / 20g. (yes)
Peas, green 5/8 lbs - 8oz / 250g. ()
Tomato 1 piece / 50g. (little)
Carrot 2 pieces / 150g. (recommended)

French beans Handful / 30g. ()
Salt 1 pinch / 1g. (little)
Pepper (ground) 1 pinch / 0,5g. ()
Parsley 1 teaspoon / 3g. (recommended)
Butter organic 1 teaspoon / 3g. (yes)

Cooking instructions:
Soak the barley in the evening for the next day. Soak the mushrooms separately at the next day. Brown onion and cumin in oil, then boil with water. Add the chopped vegetables, some salt, the barley and the shiitake mushrooms and cook everything to a thick soup. At the end, season with pepper, parsley and a little butter.

9.4 Barley soup

Diuretic, forcing spleen, supports urination, stimulates liver function, antioxidativ, promotes digestion, detoxifying, reduces blood lipids, stimulates, dissolves stagnation.
Cooking time approx. 25 min
Calories p. portion: 265
2 portions
Allergens: A

Quantity of ingredients
Barley 1 cup / 120g. (yes)
Salt 1 pinch / 1g. (little)
Ginger fresh 1/2 teaspoon / 1g. ()
Olive oil 1 table spoon / 10g. (little)
Parsley 2 table spoons / 30g. (recommended)
Water 1 1/2 cups / 240g. (yes)

Cooking instructions:
Roast the barley in the pan, then grind it to the ground, and boil with water, some salt and ginger to a mash. Before serving add oil and parsley.

Variant: You can add a better taste to the dish if you cook it with prepared vegetable or meat broth.

9.5 Basic recipe for a chicken broth worming

Strengthens blood, strengthens bone marrow, reduces blood pressure, strengthens immune system, prevents cancer, reduces radiation damage, promotes sweating, dissolves stagnation, good to fight loss of appetite, flatulence.
Cooking time approx. 2-3 hours
Calories p. portion: 90
9 portions
Allergens: L

Quantity of ingredients
Chicken meat 1/2 piece / 600g. (little)
Carrot 2 pieces / 150g. (recommended)
Leek 1 stick / 45g. ()
Celery root 1 piece / 500g. (recommended)
Ginger fresh 2 slices / 2g. ()
Fenugreek (Trigonella foenum-graecum) 1 teaspoon / 2g. (yes)
Juniper berry 1 teaspoon / 3g. (yes)
Bay leaf 3 pieces / 2g. (yes)
Water 4 cup / 900g. (yes)

Cooking instructions:
Remove chicken parts from fat. Place chicken pieces in a saucepan with hot water and heat till it boils briefly, skimming any resulting foam. Add coarsely chopped vegetables and all spices and cook over medium heat for 2 to 3 hours. Strain the finished soup. Throw away vegetables and bones.
Tip: If you want to use the meat as a soup insert, take out after 45 minutes and return only the bones in the soup.
Refrigerate for later use.

9.6 Basic recipe for a reissue soup (Congee)

Low fat content, for the drainage of the body overweight and high blood pressure.
Cooking time approx. 2-4 hours
Calories p. portion: 140
3 portions
Allergens:

Quantity of ingredients
Rice variety any 1 cup / 120g. (yes)
Water 6 cups / 700g. (yes)

Cooking instructions:
Cook rice and water in a ratio of about 1: 6. The amount of water determines the thickness of the mash (matter of taste).
Put the rice in a saucepan with a heavy lid. It is important to simmer the rice after a short boil on the slightest flame, otherwise it burns.
Boil the rice for 2-4 hours. The longer he cooks, the more he strengthens.
If you want to eat the dish for breakfast, you can put the rice on just before bedtime.
To be on the safe side, you should first check the behavior of your pot and cooker under observation for a similar amount of time, so that nothing burns.
Refrigerate for later use.

9.7 Basic recipe for a vegetable soup, nutritious

Reduces blood pressure, strengthens immune system, prevents cancer, forcing spleen, dissolves stagnation, promotes weight loss. Good to fight immunodeficiency, high blood pressure, depressions, diabetes, diarrhea, reduces blood lipids.
Cooking time approx. 2-3 hours
Calories p. portion: 48
5 portions
Allergens: L

Quantity of ingredients
Olive oil 1 table spoon / 4g. (little)
Onion white 1 piece / 60g. ()
Carrot 3 pieces / 200g. (recommended)
Parsnip 3/8 lbs - 6oz / 150g. (yes)
Celery root 1 cup / 100g. (recommended)
Ginger fresh 1/2 teaspoon / 2g. ()
Lemon 1/2 piece / 25g. ()
Juniper berry 6 pieces / 6g. (yes)
Thyme dried 1 pinch / 1g. (yes)
Lovage 1 table spoon / 3g. (recommended)
Bay leaf 2 leaves / 1g. (yes)
Salt 1 pinch / 1g. (little)
Water 3 cups / 650g. (yes)

Cooking instructions:
Cut the vegetables into cubes.
Heat oil in hot pot, fry shortly onions and vegetables.
Add cold water, then add ginger, bay leaf and lemon juice.
Season with juniper, thyme and lovage. Cover for 2 - 3 hours on a low heat and simmer.
The used vegetables should be thrown away.
The basic recipe serves as a soup base and to refine vegetables, legumes or cereals.
If you want to eat vegetable soup immediately, add the desired vegetables half an hour before.
Refrigerate for later use.

9.8 Basmati rice + Zucchini tofu dish

Diuretic, supports urination, harmonizes spleen and stomach, reduces flatulence, good to fight body overweight and high blood pressure.
Antioxidativ, promotes digestion, perspiration, reduces blood lipids, forcing spleen.
Cooking time approx. 20 min
Calories p. portion: 146
4 portions
Allergens: E

Quantity of ingredients
Soy Tofu 5/8 lbs - 8oz / 250g. (little)
Olive oil 2 table spoons / 6g. (little)
Coriander 1/2 teaspoon / 4g. (yes)
Ginger fresh 1/2 teaspoon / 4g. ()
Rice Basmati 1/2 cup / 60g. (yes)
Water 3 cups / 200g. (yes)
Zucchini 1 piece / 700g. (recommended)

Cooking instructions:
Cut tofu cubes and marinate with olive oil, tamari, crushed coriander and ginger. Leave at least 1 hour.
Cook Basmati rice with the water. You can season with onion and cardamom.
Roast zucchini and tofu in pan in the hot oil for approx. 5-7 min.
Serve rice and tofu on a plate.
Add the parsley.
Can also be used as a salad for the home and on the go.

9.9 Bath with lavender

Calming, regenerates the central nervous system. Good to fight sleep disorders, loss of appetite and nervous intestinal complaints.
Cooking time approx. 10 min
Calories p. portion: 0
2 portions
Allergens:

Quantity of ingredients
Lavender blossoms 1 sachet / 5g. (yes)

Cooking instructions:
Put a tied bag with the lavender in the water and let it soak for 10 minutes. The bag can be squeezed several times before removing it.

9.10 Buddhist reissue soup

Little laxative. Good to fight blood circulation disorders, risk of embolism, high blood pressure, a headache, heart attack and stroke.
Cooking time approx. 2-4 hours
Calories p. portion: 280
2 portions
Allergens: G

Quantity of ingredients
Rice variety any 1 cup / 120g. (yes)
Water 3 cups / 350g. (yes)
Butter organic 1 table spoon / 10g. (yes)
Honey 1 teaspoon / 3g. (little)
Cow's milk (1.5% fat) 1 cup / 120g. (yes)

Cooking instructions:
Bring the rice to boil soft in the water for for 2 to 4 hours. At the end of the cooking time add some milk, honey and butter. This basic recipe can be expanded as desired (sweet, salty). The indicated quantity is sufficient for 4 days (keep in a refrigerator)

Variant: The taste can be refined with cinnamon or vanilla.

9.11 Carrot and rice gruel soup

Stops diarrhea, good to fight fever, strengthens immune system, reduces blood pressure.
Cooking time approx. 10 min
Calories p. portion: 101
1 portions
Allergens:

Quantity of ingredients
Basic recipe for a rice soup (Congee) 1 cup / 120g. (recommended)
Carrot 2 pieces / 100g. (recommended)
Salt 1 teaspoon / 4g. (little)

Cooking instructions:
Peel and grate carrots. Heat the rice soup (according to the basic recipe) till it boils and add the grated carrots and salt. Cook for 10 minutes.

9.12 Carrots with potato foam

Promotes spleen and liver, reduces blood pressure, strengthens immune system. Improves digestion, regenerates skin, supports urination, lowers cholesterol, promotes the production of stool and urine, strengthens blood, strengthens nerves.
Cooking time approx. 30 min
Calories p. portion: 316
1 portions
Allergens: G

Quantity of ingredients
Carrot (Early Carrot) 3/8 lbs - 6oz / 150g. (recommended)
Pork meat 1/8 lbs - 2oz / 40g. (little)
Potato (mealy) 1/4 lbs - 4oz / 100g. (recommended)
Butter organic 1 table spoon / 10g. (yes)
Honey 1/2 teaspoon / 2g. (little)
Anise (Common Fennel) 1 pinch / 0,2g. (recommended)
Water 2 table spoons / 20g. (yes)

Cooking instructions:
Clean the carrots, wash thoroughly, peel thinly and cut into thin slices. Cut the meat into strips. Wash the potatoes, cook in a small saucepan

with little water in about 15 minutes.
Melt half of the butter in a saucepan, fry the carrots and the meat in it. If necessary, add 2-3 tablespoons of water, put the lid on and cook everything over low heat in about 15 minutes.
Add the honey, the anise and the remaining butter and remove the pot from the heat.
Peel the potatoes and press directly onto the plate with the potato press. Distribute the honey carrots over it.

9.13 Chicken soup with egg yolk and parsley

Strengthens blood, strengthens bone marrow, reduces blood pressure, strengthens immune system. Parsley stimulates liver function, harmonizes liver and spleen, strengthens eyesight, detoxifying.
Cooking time approx. 10 min
Calories p. portion: 118
2 portions
Allergens: CL

Quantity of ingredients
Basic recipe for a chicken soup (warming) 2 cup / 500g. (recommended)
Chicken yolk 1 piece / 10g. (little)
Parsley 1 table spoon / 10g. (recommended)

Cooking instructions:
Cook the chicken broth according to the basic recipe.
Heat broth and bubble the egg yolk. Sprinkle the chopped parsley over it and let it rest for about 2 minutes. Drink in small sips.

9.14 Compote from apples

Apple (sweet) stops diarrhea, promotes digestion, appetizing, harmonizes the stomach. Warms stomach and spleen, improves blood circulation.
Cooking time approx. 10 min
Calories p. portion: 67
2 portions
Allergens:

Quantity of ingredients
Apple (sweet) 1 piece / 220g. (little)
Water 1 1/2 cups / 220g. (yes)
Cinnamon ground 1 pinch / 1g. (yes)

Cooking instructions:
Cook the apples (organic) with the skin and seeds. Sprinkle with cinnamon.

9.15 Fennel-Rice Soup

Forcing spleen, relieves constipation, stimulates nerves, detoxifying, reduces inflammation, improves blood circulation.
Cooking time approx. 15-20 min
Calories p. portion: 156
2 portions
Allergens: EG

Quantity of ingredients
Basic recipe for a rice soup (Congee) 1 cup / 300g. (recommended)
Fennel 1/2 piece / 150g. (recommended)
Butter organic 1 table spoon / 15g. (yes)
Soy sauce 1 dash / 3g. (little)

Cooking instructions:
Cook the fennel softly in the rice soup according to the basic recipe. Before serving, add a piece of butter and some soy sauce.

9.16 Fresh full-grain porridge

Regulates gastrointestinal function. Reduces Inflammation, relieves pain, detoxifying, bactericide.
Cooking time approx. 15 min
Calories p. portion: 336
1 portions
Allergens: AG

Quantity of ingredients
Spelled wholemeal flour 1 oz / 25g. (little)
Cow's milk (whole milk 3.5% fat) 3/4 cup - 6 oz / 200g. (little)
Honey 1 teaspoon / 3g. (little)
Banana 1 piece / 120g. (recommended)

Cooking instructions:
Grind the cereal grains into a flour mill. You may also be able to use a coffee grinder, but then grind twice. Stir the flour with the milk in a saucepan and bring it to boil over medium heat. Cook the porridge on low heat for 4-5 minutes while stirring. Then add the honey. Crush the banana with a fork and pull it under the porridge.

9.17 Kohlrabi in chervil sauce with potatoes

Reduces inflammation, lowers cholesterol, diuretic, conducts bowel winds, strengthens immune system, prevents cancer, promotes weight loss. Good to fight loss of appetite, flatulence, high blood pressure, depressions, diabetes, diarrhea.
Cooking time approx. 1 hour
Calories p. portion: 188
4 portions
Allergens: GL

Quantity of ingredients
Potato 6 pieces / 450g. (recommended)
Basic recipe for a vegetable soup (nutritious) 1 cup / 300g. (recommended)
Potato 1/4 lbs - 4oz / 100g. (recommended)
Nutmeg 1 pinch / 0,2g. (yes)
Lemon peel 1/2 teaspoon / 2g. ()
Ginger fresh 1/2 teaspoon / 2g. ()
Lovage 1/2 teaspoon / 2g. (recommended)
Kohlrabi 3/4 lbs / 300g. (yes)
Salt 1 pinch / 1g. (little)
Pepper (ground) 1 pinch / 0,2g. ()
Sour cream 15% fat 2 table spoons / 30g. (yes)
Chervil dried 1 Bunch / 80g. (recommended)

Cooking instructions:
Boil the potatoes in salted water.
Bring half of the vegetable stock to boil. Add the diced potatoes, nutmeg, lemon zest, ginger and lovage. Cover the potatoes and cook for about 10 minutes until soft and puree them with a blender until they are smooth.
Bring remaining vegetable stock to boil. Cut kohlrabi into cubes and add, cover and cook for about 8 minutes. Stir in the potato sauce and heat everything briefly.
Puree with the mixing stick chervil and sour cream. Mix the chervil cream with the kohlrabi vegetables.
Serve with the cooked, peeled potatoes.

9.18 Millet mash with steamed pears

Calms stomach, strengthens tendons and bones, supports urination. Promotes digestion, supports urination. Diuretic, building up, eye-enhancing, detoxifying, nerve-strengthening.
Cooking time approx. 25 min
Calories p. portion: 235
3 portions
Allergens:

Quantity of ingredients
Millet 1 cup / 100g. (yes)
Water 1 1/2 cups / 220g. (yes)
Cardamom 1 pinch / 0,5g. (yes)
Pear 1-2 pcs. Biological / 250g. (little)
Salt 1 pinch / 0,2g. (little)
Grape juice red 1 cup / 250g. (little)
Cinnamon ground 1 pinch / 0,2g. (yes)
Clove 2 pieces / 0,4g. (yes)
Lemon juice 1 table spoon / 8g. ()

Cooking instructions:
Roast millet while stirring until it smells well.
Cool the pot briefly.
Add 2 cups of hot water, the cardamom and a pinch of salt.
On low flame, covered, for 20 min. simmer.
Quarter the pears, remove the core, peel on request, add about ¼ liter of red grape juice, cinnamon stick, cloves, lemon juice and a pinch of salt) and simmer gently covered for a few minutes.

9.19 Noodle soup

Protects the digestive system. Detoxifying, affects anorexia, reduces blood pressure, strengthens immune system, strengthens the muscles, tendons and bones. stimulates liver function, detoxifying.
Cooking time approx. 1 1/2 hours
Calories p. portion: 237
8 portions
Allergens: ACEGL

Quantity of ingredients
Beef soup meat 3/4 lbs / 300g. (little)
Water 4 cup / 900g. (yes)
Bay leaf 1 piece / 1g. (yes)
Carrot 3/4 lbs / 300g. (recommended)
Celery sticks 1 bunch / 200g. (yes)
Cauliflower 3/4 lbs / 300g. (little)
Parsley 1 Bunch / 100g. (recommended)
Noodles (wheat) with egg 3/4 lbs / 300g. (yes)
Butter organic 1 table spoon / 10g. (yes)
Salt 1 teaspoon / 2g. (little)
Soy sauce 1 table spoon / 8g. (little)
Tomato paste 1 table spoon / 10g. (little)

Cooking instructions:
Simmer the meat and bay leaf in the water over low heat for about 30 minutes.
Peel and slice the carrots.
From the celery plant separate the lower end and the leaves. Wash the stems, peel off the tough threads and cut the stems into slices about 1 cm thick.
Wash the Brussels sprouts, clean them and cut the roses from below crosswise.
Wash and chop the parsley.

Add the Brussels sprouts and carrot slices to the soup and cook for about 30 minutes.

After about 10 minutes, add the celery and green leaves and the pasta. Finally, remove the bay leaf and celery green.

(For the baby, remove about 200-250 g of carrots, celery and noodles with broth, squeeze about 35 g of meat finely and add to the baby soup, stir in the butter and 1 teaspoon of chopped parsley.)

Season the remaining soup with the salt, the soy sauce, the tomato paste and the remaining parsley. Lift out the meat. Remove fat and bones and dice the meat. Serve in the soup.

9.20 Pear compote

Promotes digestion, supports urination.
Cooking time approx. 20 min
Calories p. portion: 100
3 portions
Allergens:

Quantity of ingredients
Water 1 1/2 cups / 240g. (yes)
Pear 4 / 500g. (little)

Cooking instructions:
Halve organic pears. Cores and skin can be used. Pear in the pot and add water. Simmer for up to 20 minutes until pears are tender.

9.21 Polenta with peach

Relieves fatigue, forcing spleen, diuretic, strengthens the defense, good to fight fungi infections, lets urine and bile juice flow, prevents the aging process, strengthens brain cells.
Cooking time approx. 20 min
Calories p. portion: 197
3 portions
Allergens:

Quantity of ingredients
Water 1 1/2 cups / 240g. (yes)
Corn Grease (Polenta) 1 cup / 120g. (yes)
Peaches 2-3 pieces / 400g. (little)
Vanilla pod 1 pinch / 1g. (yes)
Cinnamon ground 1 pinch / 1g. (yes)

Cooking instructions:
Pour the polenta into a pan of hot water with constant stirring until the polenta has the desired consistency. Pull the polenta from the fire and let it soak for 10 minutes.

Wash fresh peaches and cut into quarters. Pour into the finished polenta the peaches, add the vanilla and add Chili to taste, stir and let it go for 3 minutes.

Winter varieties: Pickled fruit, pear, apples

9.22 Puréed banana

Eat 2 times a day, regulates gastrointestinal function
Cooking time approx. 7 min
Calories p. portion: 144
1 portions
Allergens:

Quantity of ingredients
Banana 1 piece / 150g. (recommended)

Cooking instructions:
Mix the banana with the fork or purée with a blender. Leave to brown for at least 5 minutes.

9.23 Quinoa with peach

Supports erythrocyte production, relieves fatigue, relaxes. Good to fight gastrointestinal complaints. Relieves pain, detoxifying, bactericide.
Cooking time approx. 20 min
Calories p. portion: 248
2 portions
Allergens:

Quantity of ingredients
Quinoa 1 cup / 100g. (yes)
Water 1 1/2 cups / 240g. (yes)
Honey 2 teaspoons / 4g. (little)
Peaches 2 pieces / 240g. (little)
Linseed oil 2 teaspoons / 4g. (little)
Lemon Balm (fresh) 1 teaspoon (chopped) / 1g. (yes)
Cinnamon ground 1 pinch / 0,2g. (yes)
Vanilla 1 pinch / 0,2g. (yes)

Cooking instructions:
In the evening:
Put quinoa in hot water and boil soft, covered 15 to 20 minutes.
In the morning:
Warm up quinoa with 1 tablespoon water.
Steam lightly Peaches in a saucepan or add them fresh. Decorate with fresh lemon balm.
Summer: nectarines, apricots
Winter: Pickled fruit, pear, apples

9.24 Rice congee with carrots and fennel

Worms, forcing spleen, relieves constipation, stimulates nerves, detoxifying, reduces inflammation, improves blood circulation, reduces blood pressure, strengthens immune system, prevents cancer, reduces radiation damage.
Cooking time approx. 2 hours and more
Calories p. portion: 131
3 portions
Allergens: G

Quantity of ingredients
Basic recipe for a rice soup (Congee) 2 cup / 500g. (recommended)
Carrot 2 pieces / 100g. (recommended)
Fennel 1 piece / 250g. (recommended)
Butter organic 1 teaspoon / 3g. (yes)
Cardamom 1/2 teaspoon / 1g. (yes)

Cooking instructions:
Cook rice congee according to basic recipe.
Clean and cut carrots and fennel.

When carrots and fennel are cooked from the beginning, they serve wholesomeness. If added shortly before the end of the cooking time, taste and vitamins are retained.

Refine with butter and cardamom before serving.

9.25 Rice congee with honey pear and black sesame

Promotes digestion, supports urination, good to fight blood circulation disorders, thromboses, risk of embolism, high blood pressure, a headache, heart attack and stroke.
Cooking time approx. 10 min - 3 hours
Calories p. portion: 158
2 portions
Allergens: N

Quantity of ingredients
Basic recipe for a rice soup (Congee) 1 1/2 cups / 240g. (recommended)
Pear 2 pieces / 300g. (little)
Sesame, black 1 teaspoon / 3g. ()

Cooking instructions:
Cook rice congee according to basic recipe.
Fill pot with 3 cm of water and heat till it boils. Quarter the pears (with the skin and seeds) and simmer them covered with black sesame for 10 minutes. Mix with the rice.

9.26 Rice dulse soup

Promotes spleen and liver, reduces blood pressure, strengthens immune system. Good to fight blood circulation disorders, diarrhea, free radicals. Antipyretic. Vitamin C rich. Promotes the exchange of iron and calcium. Increases resistance to infectious diseases.
Cooking time approx. 5 min
Calories p. portion: 190
2 portions
Allergens: L

Quantity of ingredients
Basic recipe for a rice soup (Congee) 4 cups / 500g. (recommended)
Basic recipe for a vegetable soup (nutritious) 2 cup / 500g. (recommended)
Dulse (seaweed) 2 table spoons / 15g. (yes)

Cooking instructions:
Worm up a portion of pre-cooked basic recipe for a ricesoupe (congee) and a portion pre-cooked basic recipe for a vegetable soup.
Bake the dulse in the oven at 220 degrees for 3 minutes. Spread the crisp dulse over the rice.

9.27 Rice porridge with shrubs (seeds) Yi Yi Ren

Strengths spleen and stomach, strengthens the muscles. Diuretic, supports urination.
Cooking time approx. 25 min
Calories p. portion: 212
2 portions
Allergens:

Quantity of ingredients
Water 4 cups / 450g. (yes)
Rice variety any 1 cup / 120g. (yes)
Lemon peel 1/4 piece / 2g. ()
Coix (seeds) YiYi Ren 1/2 cup / 50g. (yes)
Cress 1 table spoon / 6g. (recommended)

Cooking instructions:
Cook rice porridge according to basic recipe with a half cup of Yi Yi Ren and lemon peel. Simmer for 1 hour and then sprinkle cress over it.

9.28 Rice with parsnips

Rich in vitamins, minerals potassium and zinc. Good to fight blood circulation disorders, thrombose, risk of embolism, high blood pressure, a headache, heart attack and stroke, yeast infections.
Cooking time approx. 45 min
Calories p. portion: 206
3 portions
Allergens:

Quantity of ingredients
Rice variety any 1 cup / 120g. (yes)
Water 1 1/2 cups / 200g. (yes)
Salt 1 pinch / 1g. (little)
Parsnip 3-4 pieces / 450g. (yes)
Olive oil 1 table spoon / 10g. (little)
Sage 1 teaspoon / 3g. (yes)

Cooking instructions:
Peel the parsnips and cut into slices. Fry for a short time in oil. Add the rice and fry again for a short time. Add the water and cook it at least 30 min. Sprinkle with fresh chopped sage.

9.29 Roasted millet with Celery sticks

Promotes spleen and kidney, diuretic, promoting metabolism.
Cooking time approx. 30 min
Calories p. portion: 400
2 portions
Allergens: L

Quantity of ingredients
Millet 1 cup / 120g. (yes)
Water 1 1/2 cups / 240g. (yes)
Celery sticks 2 rods / 50g. (yes)
Herbs various 1 table spoon / 10g. (yes)
Water 2 table spoons / 30g. (yes)
Salt 1 pinch / 1g. (little)
Sage 3-4 leaves / 2g. (yes)
Cress 1 teaspoon / 3g. (recommended)

Cooking instructions:
Roast millet briefly, pour over water, heat till it boils and let stand for 20 min. to swell.

Cut celery into small pieces and mix with water, salt and fresh herbs and cook for 10 min. Add to the millet.
Sprinkle fresh sage or watercress over it.

9.30 Rosemary Potatoes

Reduces Inflammation, improves digestion, regenerates skin, supports urination, lowers cholesterol. Rosemary stimulates digestion, strengthens lung, promotes spleen and kidney, dries out.
Cooking time approx. 30 min
Calories p. portion: 188
2 portions
Allergens:

Quantity of ingredients
Potato 6-8 pieces / 420g. (recommended)
Salt (herbal) 1 pinch / 1g. (little)
Olive oil 1 table spoon / 10g. (little)
Rosemary 1 teaspoon / 2g. (yes)

Cooking instructions:
Cut the potatoes into half´s, apply a little olive oil on the cut surface, then salt, sprinkle 2 - 3 rosemary needles on the potatoes.
Place the potatoes on the baking tray and bake them in the preheated oven for approx. 25 minutes to 190°C/374°F.

9.31 Semolina porridge with banana

Regulates gastrointestinal function, reduces inflammation, antiallergic, good to fight blood circulation disorders.
Cooking time approx. 15 min
Calories p. portion: 307
1 portions
Allergens: AG

Quantity of ingredients
Cow's milk (whole milk 3.5% fat) 3/4 cup - 6 oz / 200g. (little)
Spelled semolina 2 table spoons / 30g. (yes)
Butter organic 1 teaspoon / 4g. (yes)
Banana 1/2 piece / 50g. (recommended)

Cooking instructions:
Heat the half of the milk in a small pot. Add the semolina and boil it shortly in the milk. Let it swell at low heat for 3 minutes with constant stirring. Remove the pot from the heat, add the remaining milk with the snow bean and place the mush in a small bowl. Add the butter and the battered banana.
For adults, a pinch of cinnamon can be spread over it.

9.32 Spring vegetables

Diuretic, supports urination, supports digestion. Diuretic, harmonizes the stomach and intestines, conducts bowel winds, strengthens immune system.
Cooking time approx. 1 1/2 hour
Calories p. portion: 64
8 portions
Allergens: G

Quantity of ingredients
Carrot 1,1 lbs / 500g. (recommended)
Kohlrabi 1,1 lbs / 500g. (yes)
Butter organic 2 table spoons / 20g. (yes)
Water 1/2 cup / 125g. (yes)

Cooking instructions:
Wash the vegetables thoroughly. Clean and peel carrots and turnip cabbage. From the turnip cabbage, finely chop some delicate leaves and set aside. Rasp the carrots and the turnip cabbage. Melt the butter, add the water and the vegetables and cook over medium heat for about 30 minutes. Stir occasionally. Spread the vegetables and cooked water to about 8 deep-frozen bags to a100-150 g (depending on the age of the child). Close the bags, allow them to cool down and freeze them for max 3 months.
If necessary thaw, boil and mix with 80g of boiled potatoes and an egg. (The recipe can easily be varied if you want to use cauliflower, peas or zucchini)

9.33 Tea from anise

Anise (wild fennel) promotes digestion, forcing spleen and stomach.
Cooking time approx. 15 min
Calories p. portion: 3
4 portions
Allergens:

Quantity of ingredients
Anise (Common Fennel) 1 teaspoon / 3g. (recommended)
Water 2 cup / 500g. (yes)

Cooking instructions:
Heat the water till it boils and put it aside. Add anise.
10 min. to let go.
Pour through a tea strainer. Sweet to taste with honey.

In order to achieve a salutary effect, you should drink 2 cups of anise tea per day.

9.34 Tea from blue mallow

Good to fight stomach pain, gastritis.
Cooking time approx. 10 min
Calories p. portion: 0
2 portions
Allergens:

Quantity of ingredients
Blue mallow tee 2 table spoons / 14g. (recommended)
Water 2 cup / 500g. (yes)

Cooking instructions:
Heat the water till it boils and put it aside. Add cheesecloth tea and 10 min. to let go. Sweet to taste with honey.
Strain when pouring.

9.35 Tea from chamomile

Good to fight flatulence, nausea, intestinal cramps, diarrhea, inflammation of the oral mucosa, influenza infections, stomach and intestinal mucosa infections, badly healing wounds, nausea, colds, skin rashes, inflammation in the genital and anal area.

Cooking time approx. 10 min
Calories p. portion: 0
1 portions
Allergens:

Quantity of ingredients
Chamomile 1 teaspoon / 3g. (yes)
Water 1 cup / 120g. (yes)

Cooking instructions:
Heat the water till it boils and put it aside. Chamomile flowers added and 10 min. to let go.

9.36 Tea from fennel

Harmonizes stomach, less bloating.
Cooking time approx. 10 min
Calories p. portion: 0
4 portions
Allergens:

Quantity of ingredients
Fennel tea 2 table spoons / 20g. (recommended)
Water 2 cup / 500g. (yes)

Cooking instructions:
Heat the water till it boils and put it aside. Add fennel tea and 10 min. to let go. Sweet to taste with honey. Strain when pouring.

9.37 Tea from mallow

Relieves irritation cough, soothes mucous membranes in mouth, throat, stomach and intestines, inhibits inflammation, easily contracting (astringent).
Cooking time approx. 10 min
Calories p. portion: 0
4 portions
Allergens:

Quantity of ingredients
Mallow (Malva sylvestris) blossom tea 2 teabags / 4g. (yes)
Water 2 cup / 500g. (yes)

Cooking instructions:
Heat the water till it boils and put it aside. Add mallow tee and 10 min. to let go. Sweet to taste with honey. Strain when pouring.

9.38 Tea from mugwort

Reduces Bleeding, relieves pain, makes fat food easier to digest.
Cooking time approx. 10 min
Calories p. portion: 0
2 portions
Allergens:

Quantity of ingredients
Water 2 cup / 500g. (yes)

Cooking instructions:
Heat the water till it boils and put it aside. Add mugwort and 10 min. to let go. Sweet to taste with honey.

9.39 Tea Green tea

Green tea promotes digestion, supports urination, dissolves mucus, detoxifying, stimulates nerves, reduces blood lipids, lowers cholesterol, reduces inflammation.
Cooking time approx. 10 min
Calories p. portion: 2
1 portions
Allergens:

Quantity of ingredients
Green tea 1 teaspoon / 2g. (yes)
Water 1 cup / 120g. (yes)

Cooking instructions:
For each cup you use a teaspoonful or a teabag.
Pour green tea only with 60 to 80 ° C / 140 to 176 °F hot water, otherwise it will be bitter.
If the tea has a stimulating effect, let it draw for two to three minutes. It has a calming effect for a duration of five minutes (no longer, otherwise it will be bitter!).
Another method: Pour the tea leaves with about 70 ° C / 158 °F hot water and pour the water immediately again.
Then just pour hot water again. The bitter substances disappear and the tea gets a milder aroma.

9.40 Tea stomach tea

Promotes digestion.
Cooking time approx. 15 min
Calories p. portion: 3
2 portions
Allergens:

Quantity of ingredients
Fennel seeds ground 1 teaspoon / 2g. (recommended)
Licorice root tea 2 pieces / 3g. (yes)
Water 1 cup / 250g. (yes)

Cooking instructions:
Put fennel seeds lightly pounded into a kettle with the licorice. Boil water for about 2 minutes and pour into the kettle. Leave for 10 min and strain.
(For baby's cool down hand warm and put it in a bottle).

9.41 Tender fennel vegetables

Relieves constipation, stimulates nerves, reduces inflammation, improves blood circulation, regenerates skin, supports urination.
Promotes digestion.
Cooking time approx. 25 min
Calories p. portion: 70
2 portions
Allergens: G

Quantity of ingredients
Potato 1 piece / 50g. (recommended)
Fennel 1/4 lbs - 4oz / 100g. (recommended)
Water 2 table spoons / 20g. (yes)
Butter organic 1 table spoon / 10g. (yes)

Cooking instructions:
Wash the potato and peel with a peeler. Cut into cubes of about 2 cm. Wash the fennel, remove stained, dark spots and cut the tuber. Heat till it boils with 2 tablespoons of water in a small saucepan. Cook on low heat for about 15 minutes. Fish out the caraway seeds. Puree the vegetables with the blender and stir in the butter.
Fennel and caraway soothe the stomach and prevent bloating. In addition, fennel contains a lot of vitamin C and folic acid. An ideal meal for sick children.

10 Effects of food

10.1 Use ingredients: recommendable

Acai powder
Aloe juice
Anise (Common Fennel)
Asparagus (green or white)
Aubergine
Banana
Banana (cooking banana)
Basic recipe for a beef soup
Basic recipe for a beef soup (warming)
Basic recipe for a chicken soup (warming)
Basic recipe for a fish soup
Basic recipe for a rice soup (Congee)
Basic recipe for a vegetable soup (nutritious)
Bitter Herb liqueur
Black caraway
Blackberry´s
Blue mallow tee
Cantaloupe
Carrot
Carrot (Early Carrot)
Carrot juice without sugar
Celery root
Chamomile tea
Chervil
Chervil dried
Chinese pearl barley
Codfish
Cottage cheese
Cream 10% coffee cream
Cress
Crucian
Dill
Elderberries
Elderberry blossom tee
Fennel
Fennel seeds ground
Fennel tea
Fox nut, gorgon nut, makhana
Gourd
Ground
Ground caraway
Herbal tea mix
Hibiscus
Hokkaido pumpkin
Kudzu
Lamb's lettuce
Lily bulbs
Loquate / Japanese medlar
Lotus roots
Lotus seeds
Lovage
Mascarpone cheese
Parsley
Parsley root
Potato
Potato (mealy)
Pumpkin
Red beet
Spinach
Turnips
Watermelon
Wax gourd
Zucchini

10.2 Use ingredients: yes

Amaranth
Amaranth Pops
Angelica root
Apple puree
Arrowroot
Artichoke
Baking powder
Balm
Bamboo shoots
Banchatee (green tea)
barberry
Barley
Barley flour
Barley grass powder
Barley grouts
Barley malt
Barley not peeled
Basil
Basil (fresh)
Batavia
Bay leaf
Berries of the season
Blackberry leaves
Blueberry
Borage
Boxhorn clover seeds

Bread roll
Bread with carob kernel flour
Breadcrumbs (wheat bread, bread roll)
Broccoli
Buckbean
Buckwheat
Buckwheat (roasted) Kasha
Bulgur (cereals)
Burdock root tea
Butter (half fat)
Butter organic
Buttermilk
Calamari
Carambola (Star fruit)
Cardamom
Carob flour, St. john's bread
Celery sticks
Cereal coffee
Chamomile
Channa-Dal
Chard
Chicken egg white
Chickweed
Chicory
Chlorella (fresh water)
Chrysanthemum blossom tea
Cinnamon ground
Cinnamon sticks
Clove
Cod
Coix (seeds) YiYi Ren
Compote (fruits of the season)
Coriander
Coriander (fresh)
Corn
Corn (fast polenta)
Corn (roasted)
Corn flour
Corn Grease (Polenta)
Corn silk tea
Corn starch
Couscous
Cow's milk (1.5% fat)
Crab
Cranberry
Cranberry
Cranberry jam
Cranberry juice
Cream sour 10%
Creamer
Crispbread
Cumin (Caraway seed)
Curcuma
Curd cheese 20%
Currant (black)
Currant (red)
Currant (white)
Daisy
Dandelion (young plants)
Dandelion juice
Dandelionroots tea
Dashi
Dulse (seaweed)
Endive salad
Fenugreek (Trigonella foenum-graecum)
Feta cheese
Fig
Fish pieces mixed (fresh water)
Flounder
Flower pollen
Freshwater crab
Freshwater fish
Fruit tea
Galangal
Gelatin white
Gelee Royal
Gentian root
Gentian root tea
Ginkgo fruit
Ginseng
Ginseng root
Goat and sheep's milk
Goat cheese
Gooseberry
Green tea
Guava
Halibut (Flatfish)
Hawthorn
Herbs bitter
Herbs of Provence
Herbs various
Herbs wild
Hibiscus tea
Hijiki
Hyssop
Iceberg lettuce
Jasmine blossoms tee
Jellyfish
Juniper berry
Kalmus
Kefir
King Solomon's-seal
Kohlrabi
Kukicha tea
Kumquats
Ladyfingers
Lamb's lettuce

Lavender blossoms
Leaf salads (bitter)
Lemon Balm (dried)
Lemon Balm (fresh)
Lemongrass
Lettuce
Licorice root tea
Lime blossom tea
Liver smoothing tea
Lobster
Longane
Lovage seeds
Luo Han Guo fruit
Lychee
Lychee in Preserved
Lye roll
Mallow (Malva sylvestris) blossom tea
Mare's milk
Marjoram
Mediterranean fish (cod, plaice, haddock, sea eel, mackerel)
Medlar
Millet
Millet flakes
Mineral water
Miso
Miso black (fermented)
Mulberry fruit
Mulled Wine Spice
Mullet
Mussels
Nasturtium (nose-twister or nose-tweaker)
Nettles
Noodles (wheat) with egg
Noodles (wheat, lasagne) with egg
Noodles (wheat, ribbon noodles) with egg
Noodles (wheat, spaghetti) with egg
Nori, purple seaweed, red algae
Nutmeg
Oat
Oat flour
Oat fusion (baby food)
Oat milk
Octopus
Octopus
Okra
Orange blossom
Oregano dried
Oregano fresh
Oysters
Papaya
Parsnip
Passion blossoms tea
Passion fruit
Pearl barley
Pearl barley
Peppermint
Peppermint tea
Perch
Pimento
Plaice
Pomegranate
Potato flour
Prickly pear
Processed cheese 12%
Pudding powder vanilla
Quince
Quinoa
Radicchio
Radish black
Radish leaves
Raspberry
Raspberry leaf tea
Red berry (without sugar)
Rhubarb
Ribworttea
Rice (fragrance)
Rice (Gaoliang / Sorghum)
Rice Basmati
Rice flour
Rice long grain rice
Rice malt
Rice mash
Rice noodles
Rice red
Rice round grain
Rice starch
Rice sticky
Rice sweet
Rice variety any
Romaine lettuce / lettuce salad
Rose blossom tea
Rose hip
Rose hip tea
Rose leaf tea
Rosefish
Rosemary
Rucola
Rusk
Rye
Rye flour
Safflower (Dyer's thistle / Hong Hua)
Saffron
Sage
Sago (cereals)
Salmon

Salsify
Sea buckthorn
Seacrab
Shark
Sheep's milk
Sheep's milk yoghurt
Shrimp
Shrimps
Skim milk powder
Slug
Sorrel
Sour cream 15% fat
Sour milk
Sour milk cheese 20%
Sourdough
Spelled flakes
Spelled grain
Spelled semolina
Spiny lobsters
Spurdog (spiny dogfish, Schillerlocken)
Star anise
Stevia (candyleaf, sweetleaf)
Strawberries
Sugar substitute (sweetener)
Supplementary nutrition
Sweet potato
Tarragon (Estragon)
Tea mixture uric acid lowering
Thyme
Thyme dried
Topinambur
Trout
Tsampa (roasted barley flour)
Turmeric (yellow root)
Turnip
Valerian
Vanilla
Vanilla pod
Vanilla powder
Wakame
Water
Water hot
Wheat
Wheat bulgur
Wheat flakes
Wheat flatbread/pita bread
Wheat flour
Wheat semolina
Wheat semolina for children
Wheatgrass juice
Wheatgrass powder
Whey
White bread (baguette)
White bread (pretzel sticks)
White bread (roll)
White bread (wheat bread)
White breadcrumbs
White dumpling bread (wheat bread cut into chunks)
Whitefish
Wild herbs
Wild strawberries
Wormwood herb
Yam root, yam root tuber
Yarrow
Yarrow tea
Yogi tea
Yogurt (natural, 1.5% fat)

10.3 Use ingredients: little

Acerola fruit nectar or powder
Agar agar (kelp)
Agave nectar
Apple (sour)
Apple (sweet)
Apple juice (natural cloudy)
Apricot jam
Avocado
Bean oil
Bearberry leaf
Beef fillet
Beef meat
Beef meat (calf)
Beef meatbones
Beef Oxtail pieces
Beef soup meat
Berry juice
Blackberry jam
Blueberry dried
Blueberry jam
Blueberry juice
Borage oil
Buckwheat whole grain
Capers in olive oil
Cauliflower
Caviar
Chestnut puree
Chestnuts
Chicken egg
Chicken meat
Chicken yolk
Clarified butter

Cocoa
Cooking oil
Corn germ oil
Cow's milk (whole milk 3.5% fat)
Cranberries
Cream sour 20%
Cucumber
Cucumber (bitter)
Cucumber (spicy cucumber)
Curd cheese 40%
Currant jam (black)
Currant jam (red)
Currant juice (black)
Currants (black)
Currants (red)
Dates dried
Dates red
Deer meat
Deer meat
Deer's Bones
Ducks egg
Edam cheese
Feta cheese
Fig dried
Fish innards
Fish remains
Fish sauce
Fresh cheese
Fresh cheese from soya
Fresh cheese with herbs
Fructose (glucose)
Fruit mix juice
Goat
Goose egg
Gouda cheese
Grape juice red
Grape juice white
Grapes red
Grapes white
Grapeseed oil
Grass carp
Green spelt
Herring
Honey
Hop
Horse meat
Kiwi
Kombu seaweed (Saccharina japonica)
Lamb bones
Lamb meat
Lamb shoulder
Linseed oil
Mackerel
Malt
Mango
Mango juice
Maple syrup
Margarine
Margarine (diet)
Mold cheese
Mozzarella
Multi-grain bread (gray bread)
Mustard seeds
Mutton
Mutton
Nectarine
Oat flakes roasted
Oat meal
Olive oil
Orange jam
Palm oil
Peaches
Peaches (canned)
Peanut oil
Pear
Pear juice
Pheasant
Pigeon
Pigeon egg
Pineapple
Pineapple (from a can)
Pineapple juice without sugar
Poppy
Pork ham
Pork ham cooked
Pork ham smoked
Pork knuckle
Pork meat
processed cheese 30%
Pumpkin seed oil
Quail
Quail egg
Rabbit
Rabbit (wild)
Rabbit meat
Raisins
Rapeseed oil
Raspberry dried (immature)
Raspberry jam
Salt
Salt (herbal)
Sesame oil
Soy flour
Soy noodles
Soy sauce
Soy Tofu
Soy Tofu smoked
Soybean milk

Soybean oil
Spelled (Dark) bread
Spelled wholemeal flour
St. Benedict's thistle, blessed thistle, holy thistle, spotted thistle
Strawberry jam
Strawberry Juice
Sugar - icing sugar
Sugar brown
Sugar candy white
Sugar cane sugar
Sugar fructose - fruit sugar
Sugar glucose - grapes sugar
Sugar Milk Sugar
Sugar molasses
Sugar palm sugar
Sugar white
Sunflower oil
Thistle oil
Tomato
Tomato juice
Tomato paste
Tomato puree
Tonic Water
Truffle
Tuna
Turkey breast meat
Turkey ham
Umeboshi paste
Vanilla sugar natural
Vegetable juice
Vinegar (Apple vinegar)
Vinegar (Red wine vinegar)
Vinegar Aceto Balsamico
Vinegar Aceto Balsamico white
Walnut oil
Wheat germ oil
Wild boar meat
Yeast
Yoghurt vanilla
Yogurt (natural, 3.5% fat)

10.4 Do not use contra-acting foods

Adzuki beans
Agrimony
Almond
Almond marzipan
Almond milk
Almond puree
Anchovy / Sardine
Apricot
Apricot dried
Apricot nectar
Apricots
Apricots juice
Basic recipe for a duck soup
Beans (green, fresh)
Beef bone marrow
Beef heart
Beef heart (calf)
Beef kidney
Beef liver
Beef lungs (calf)
Beef stomach
Beer (alcohol-free)
Beer (alcohol-reduced)
Beer (Pils)
Beer (Top-fermented German dark beer)
Bitter Lemon
Bitter liqueur
Bitter orange peel
Black beans
Black fungus mushroom
Black tea
Blackberry dried (unripe fruit)
Black-eyed peas
Blackthorn (Sloe)
Bocksdorn fruits (Fructus Lycii, Goji, goji berry
Boletus mushroom
Brazil nuts
Brie cheese
Broad beans (thick beans)
Brown ale
Brussels sprouts
Bush beans
Butter beans white
Camembert
Campari
Carp
Cashews
Champignon
Chanterelle
Chenpi (chinese tangerine bowl)
Cherry
Cherry (sour)
Cherry compote
Cherry juice
Chicken Blood
Chicken heart
Chicken liver
Chicken stomach

Chickpeas
Chili (pod or ground)
Chinese cabbage
Chives
Chocolate
Chocolate (Diabetic)
Clementine
Clementines
Coconut fat
Coconut flakes
Coconut grated
Coconut meat
Coconut milk
Coffee
Cola drink
Cola drink (low calorie)
Cream (30% fat)
Cream sour 30%
Cream, sweet 30%
Créme fraiche cheese
Curry
Curry paste red
Deer's kidneys
Duck (heart)
Duck (slaughtered)
Dyer's broom herb
Eel
Eel smoked
Emmental cheese
Evening primrose oil
Fernet Branca (herbal bitter liqueur)
French beans
Gail plum
Garam Masala powder
Garlic
Ginger fresh
Ginger oil
Ginger powder
Ginseng liqueur
Goat and sheep's blood
Goat and sheep's brain
Goat and sheep's liver
Goat and sheep's stomach
Goose
Goose blood
Goose fat
Goose parts
Gorgonzola
Grapefruit (Pomelo)
Grapefruit dried peel
Grapefruit juice
Greengage
Hazelnuts
Honey wine (Met)
Horehound leaves
Kaki plum
Kidney beans (red)
Lamb kidneys
Lamb liver
Leek
Lemon
Lemon juice
Lemon peel
Lentils
Lentils black
Lentils red
Lentils yellow
Lima beans
Lime
Linseed
Linseed (crushed)
Lychee liqueur
Manioc flour
Martini
Mayonnaise 50%
Mayonnaise 80%
Mirabelle plum
Miso paste (soy bean paste)
Mixed Pickles
Morel (black, dried)
Morel, dried
Mu Erh Mushroom
Muesli
Mung bean
Mung bean sprouting
Mustard
Mustard Dijon
Mustard medium hot
Mustard sweet
Noodles (whole grain) with egg
Oat flakes (whole grain)
Olives
Olives green
Onion (shallot)
Onion (spring onion)
Onion read
Onion white
Orange
Orange dried peel
Orange grated peel
Orange juice
Orange peel
Oyster mushroom
Oyster shell powder
Parmesan
Peanut (roasted)
Peanut butter
Peanuts

Peas
Peas, green
Pepper (ground)
Pepper Cayenne
Pepper powder (hot)
Pepper white (ground)
Peppercorns
Pepperoni
Pepperoni, red, pitted, halved
Pepperoni, yellow, pitted, halved
Peppers
Peppers (rose peppers)
Peppers (sweet)
Peppers powder
Pickle
Pig blood
Pine nuts
Pinto beans speckled
Pistachios
Plum
Plum dried
Plums
Pork Bacon
Pork brain
Pork fat (lard)
Pork heart
Pork kidneys
Pork Lard
Pork liver
Pork lung
Pork marrow bones
Pork sausage (Bratwurst)
Pork skin
Pork stomach
Pork/beef sausage (smoked)
Pork's intestine
Prosecco
Psyllium seed
Puff pastry
Pumpernickel (dark bread)
Pumpkin seeds
Rabbit liver
Radish
Radish (white, green, purple-red)
Radish horseradish
Red cabbage
Red wine
Reishi mushroom
Rice (whole grain)
Rice black
Rice wild (nature rice)
Rum
Rye wholemeal bread
Sake
Sauerkraut (cutted cabbage fermented)
Savory
Savoy cabbage / kale
Sea cucumber
Sesame oil roasted
Sesame paste (Tahini)
Sesame, black
Sesame, white
Sherry (whine)
Shiitake, dried
Sour cherries
Soya Cuisine (soy cream)
Soybeans
Soybeans, black
Soybeans, blacks, fermented
Soybeans, yellow
Spirit
Sunflower seeds
Tabasco
Tangerine
Toast bread (whole grain)
Tomato dried
Trout (smoked)
Umeboshi plums (Japanese apricots)
Walnuts
Walnuts roasted
Wheat beer
Wheat bran
Wheat flour whole grain
Wheat/Rye/Gray-black bread with yeast
White beans
White cabbage
White wine
Whole grain bread
Wholemeal flour
Wild garlic (garlic spinach)
Wormwood
Yew nut

11 Herbs and their effects

11.1 Mugwort

Reduces bleeding, alleviates pain. In the kitchen, mugwort is used as a spice for fat food. Since it contains many bitter substances, it boosts fat burning and promotes digestion.

11.2 Chamomile

Antispasmodic and anti-inflammatory for digestive disorders, soothes the nerves and promotes good sleep. Applied externally, it heals wounds in the mouth-throat area and the skin. Strengthens eyesight.

11.3 Chervil dried

Forces urination, detoxifying, blood-purifying and blood-pressure-reducing effects.

11.4 Coriander

The essential oils are appetizing, digestive, cramping and soothing in stomach and intestinal disorders.

11.5 Herbs various

Appetizing, lots of trace elements and vitamins

11.6 Cress

Diuretic, supports urination. Good to fight dry mouth, inner agitation, sore throat, diabetes, kidney stones, gastrointestinal complaints, lung problems, menstrual cramps or cancer.

11.7 Lavender blossoms

Calms the central nervous system, relieves anxiety, to fight sleep disturbances, loss of appetite and nervous intestinal complaints.

11.8 Lovage

Stimulates digestion, reduces pain. Extracts of the root are used to flush out urinary tract infections and prevent kidney gravel.

11.9 Parsley

Stimulates liver function, detoxifies. Forces urinating. Relieves flatulence. Digestive and menstrual stimulating, birth-accelerating, memory-enhancing, blood-purifying, skin-smoothing.

11.10 Rosemary

Promotes digestion, relieves bloating, strengthens lung, spleen and kidney. Affects the circulation and nerves. Appetizing. Baths help to fight circulatory disorders as well as with gout and rheumatism.

11.11 Sage

Good to fight yeast infections. The leaves have a digestive effect and are used in greasy foods. Antiperspirant effect. Helps to relieve coughing attacks. Dries out (TCM).

11.12 Thyme dried

Disinfecting. It stimulates the blood circulation, increases the appetite and helps to digest fat meat better. Strengthens lungs and spleen (TCM).

11.13 Lemon Balm (fresh)

Stimulating, antibacterial, encouraging, relaxing, antispasmodic, cooling, antipyretic, analgesic, sweat-inducing, virus-inhibiting. Good for colds, fever, flu, cough, bronchitis, asthma, loss of appetite, bloating, heartburn.

12 Basics of Nutrition

The basic principles of nutrition described herein are general recommendations. They are not aimed at a specific form of therapy. Recommendations concerning a therapy have priority.

12.1 Nutrition

Regular meals in a relaxed atmosphere. A warm breakfast is considered a good start into the day.
The main meals ought to be taken for lunch – supper in the early evening. Pay attention to feeling hungry or sated: don't eat too much nor remain hungry is the rule
Prepare the meals freshly from natural, regional products. Frozen, heat-conserved, industrially prepared or foodstuffs cooked in the microwave oven are rejected.
Choice of foodstuffs according to the season: more cooling food in summer, more warming food in winter.
Eat cooked food at least twice a day. Food and drinks ought to be lukewarm, never ice-cold or hot.
Raw vegetables, briefly cooked vegetables, freshly squeezed juices and mineral water are not recommended. Milk and dairy products are only included in the diet if they don't cause problems.
Don't use therapeutic recipes over a longer period without consulting your doctor or therapist.

Varied food
Enjoy the diversity of foodstuffs. Characteristics of a balanced nutrition are variety, suitable combination and a balanced quantity of rich and low energy foodstuffs (on one hand avoiding undersupply with essential nutrients and on the other hand to take to many undesirable substances).

A lot of Cereal Products - and Potatoes
Bread, pasta, rice, cereal flakes (best wholemeal) as well as potatoes contain almost no fat, but many vitamins, mineral nutrients, trace elements, roughage and secondary plant substances. These foodstuffs ought to be taken with low-fat side dishes.

Vegetables and Fruit – „Take Five“ every day …
5 portions of vegetables and fruit a day, as fresh as possible, briefly cooked, or maybe one portion as a juice – ideal as a side dish to every meal as well as snack between meals: Thus a lot of vitamins, mineral nutrients as well as roughage and secondary plant substances

Daily milk and dairy products

Milk and Dairy Products every Day, once or twice per Week Fish; meat, sausages as well as eggs moderately. These foodstuffs contain valuable nutrients like calcium in the milk, iodine selenium and omega-3 fat acids in saltwater fish. Meat is favorable due to its high content of disposable iron and the vitamins B1, B6 and B12. Quantities of 300 – 600 g meat and sausage per week are sufficient. Prefer low-fat products, especially in meat- and dairy products.

Low-fat and fatty Foodstuffs

Fat supplies us with essential fat acids and fatty foodstuffs contain also fat-soluble vitamins. Fat is high in energy; therefore much fat in the food may cause overweight, possibly also cancer. Too many saturated fat acids may further a tendency for cardio-vascular diseases in the long term. Prefer vegetable oils and fats (e.g. rapeseed-, olive-, soya-oils and solid fats produced therefrom). Beware of invisible fat in meat- and dairy products, pastry and sweets as well as in fast-food and convenience foods. 70 – 90 g fat per day is sufficient.

Moderately Sugar and Salt

Take sugar and foods/drinks containing various kinds of sugar (e.g. glucose syrup) only occasionally. Use herbs and spices as well as a little salt creatively. Prefer salt containing iodine.

Plenty of Liquids

Water is absolutely essential. Drink 1-2 l liquids every day. Prefer water (with or without gas) and other low-calorie drinks. Alcoholic drinks should not be taken.

Tasty Dishes, carefully cooked

Cook the meals with as low temperatures and as short as possible, using little water and fat – this preserves the original taste, keeps the nutrients intact and prevents the production of harmful compounds.

Take time and enjoy the food

Take your Time and enjoy your Food
Eating consciously helps to eat right. The eye enjoys food, too. It's fun, invites to enjoy varied dishes and stimulates the feeling of satiety.

Watch your Weight and stay in Motion

A balanced diet and a lot of exercise and sport (30 – 60 min/day) are a healthy combination. The right weight furthers well-being and health. Thermals, directional effectiveness, digestive power

There are various criteria for judging the effectiveness of herbs and foodstuffs.
The use of certain herbs and ingredients is based on observations of the effects on the body which these foodstuffs, herbs and spices show after having eaten them. The medical science has developed following system: Every ingredient or herb has a directional effectiveness. Furthermore, there are herbs which have a special effect on certain organs.
The basic condition for a healthy metabolism is to obtain sufficient energy from food and that the digestive process doesn't use too much energy. An easily digestible meal makes content and sated, doesn't cause flatulence and fatigue after the meal. The perfect spices increase the healthiness of our meals. Very often, just small doses of herbs and spices will suffice. They are not used to make us sated, but to help our digestive organs to digest the food.

12.2 Recipes

The recipes list the ingredients to be used and the cooking instructions show how the dish is prepared. The list of ingredients shows the concerned quantities as well as the relevance for the therapy. If you find „less than mentioned“, try to comply or find an alternative from the „list of recommended foodstuffs“. Mostly it shall result just in a small change of taste when you simply avoid this ingredient.
Mild cooking methods: boiling, stewing, poaching, steaming
Strong cooking methods: barbecuing, roasting, frying, smoking
Balanced cooking methods: deep-frying, baking brick
Deep-freezing and warming in the microwave oven should be avoided (denaturalization).

12.3 Foodstuffs

Foodstuffs have an effect on body and soul like medicinal herbs, only a very much milder one. Dietary advice is mainly based on regional foodstuffs. The knowledge about the effects of each foodstuff and the knowledge, when which foodstuff shall be used, is based on the orthodox school of medicine. Use ecologic-organic products, if possible. As everything should be cooked for a long time due to a better digestability and very rarely eaten raw, the food agrees with everyone.
The classification of the foodstuffs according to their effect on the body is the basis in order to achieve a harmonious status of health.

Dietary advisors do not recommend certain foodstuffs for everyone. The individual diet is tailor-made for the individual constitution.

Buy only fresh and ripe fruit and vegetables. You ought to leave unripe fruit and vegetables and such with brown spots and wilted leaves behind in the market. In this case take deep-frozen goods (never ready-to-serve dishes!). Fruit and vegetables are deep-frozen immediately after harvesting and often contain more vitamins and minerals than the goods from the vegetable shelf. Whereas conserved or tinned goods contain very much less biological substances. Also, salt, sugar and others are mostly added to the latter. Never leave the foodstuffs in the water after washing them to avoid that many vital substances get drowned. Clean salads, fruit and vegetables immediately before serving.

Please make sure of the hygienic processing of foodstuffs. Clean your salads, fruit and vegetables carefully. When cooking with meat, prepare all ingredients first and then process the meat products. Clean the worktop and tools very carefully. Wooden surfaces ought to be treated with a mild disinfectant regularly in order to reduce germination.

Store fruit and vegetables separately, if possible. Harvested fruit and vegetables are still alive and emit e.g. ethylene gas, which makes other products ripen and age faster. Keep meat and fish in the closed packaging or store them in the fridge in closed containers.

12.4 Herbs

There are some basic rules for storing medicinal herbs. On principle, herbs must be protected from direct sunlight, humidity and heat.

Containers for the storage of herbs may be glasses, ceramic jars and even plastic containers. However, plastic is a rather unsuitable material and should only be a short-term solution. In case of glass containers, use a dark material.

Medicinal herbs cannot be kept for any long period. The shelf life of herbs is limited. However, it can be prolonged with suitable storage. The place should be dark, rather cool and absolutely dry. A wooden medicine cabinet, placed not directly next to a source of heat, would be ideal. Never buy large quantities of herbs so as not to have to throw them away. Label the container with the name of the herb and the date of harvesting or processing.

13 Other dietic-books

The following syndromes of dietetics, TCM or for a therapy supplement for cancer are available.

Dietetics

E001. Nutrition of the infant - baby food
E002. Nutrition during lactation
E003. Nutrition in old age
E004. Nutrition of children and adolescents
E005. Nutrition of athletes
E006. Light weight
E007. Pregnancy
E008. Full food

Protein and electrolyte - kidneys
E009. (hemodialysis) dialysis treatment
E010. Acute renal failure
E011. Chronic renal insufficiency
E012. Nephrotic syndrome
E013. Kidney stones (nephrolithiasis)

Gastrointestinal tract - pancreas
E014. Acute pancreatitis (inflammation of the pancreas)
E015. Chronic pancreatitis (inflammation of the pancreas)

Gastrointestinal tract - small intestine and large intestine
E016. Acute obstipation (constipation)
E017. Chronic obstipation (constipation)
E018. Colon irritabile
E019. Diverticulitis
E020. Acquired lactose intolerance (lactose malabsorption)
E021. Fructose malabsorption
E022. Glutensensitive enteropathy (celiac disease)
E023. Colectomy
E024. Short Bowel Syndrome

Gastrointestinal tract - liver, gallbladder, bile ducts
E025. Acute and chronic hepatitis (inflammation of the liver)
E026. Cholelithiasis (bile stones)
E027. fatty liver
E028. cirrhosis

Gastrointestinal tract - Stomach and duodenal intestine
E029. Acute gastritis
E030. Chronic gastritis
E031. Stomach bleeding
E032. Ulcus ventriculi and duodenal ulcer
E033. Condition after gastric surgery

Gastrointestinal tract - oral cavity and esophagus
E034. Stomatitis
E035. Esophageal carcinoma (esophageal cancer)
E036. Refluosophagitis (heartburn)

Special diseases
E037. Phenylketonuria (PKU)
E038. Rheumatic joint diseases

Metabolism
E039. Obesity (overweight)
E040. Diabetes mellitus
E041. Eating disorders (underweight)

Fat metabolism
E042. Hypercholesterolaemia (increased cholesterol level)
E043. Hepatic Encephalopathy

Heart and circulation
E044. Arteriosclerosis (arterial calcification)
E045. Heart insufficiency
E046. Hypertension
E047. Hyperuricaemia and gout

Changed nutrient requirements
E048. In case of fever
E049. For malignant diseases
E050. After burns
E051. Radiation and chemotherapy

CANCER
E100. Pancreatic cancer
E101. Bladder cancer
E102. Blood cancer (leukemia)
E103. Breast cancer
E104. Colorectal cancer
E105. Gastric cancer
E106. Kidney cancer
E107. Esophageal cancer

TCM
E200. Bladder - moisture heat in the bladder
E201. Bladder - moisture and cold in the bladder
E202. Bladder - emptiness and cold in the bladder
E203. Large intestine - external cold affects the large intestine
E204. Large intestine - moisture heat in the large intestine
E205. Large intestine - heat blocks the intestine II acute
E206. Large intestine - dryness of the colon
E207. Large intestine - Yang deficiency (cold)
E208. Heart - Blood insufficiency
E209. Heart - Blood stagnation
E210. Heart - Fire
E211. Heart - Hot mucus clogs the heart pores

E212. Heart - Cold mucus clogs the heart pores
E213. Heart - Qi deficiency
E214. Heart - Yang deficiency
E215. Heart - Yin deficiency
E216. Liver - Ascending Liver Yang
E217. Liver - Blood deficiency
E218. Liver - Blood stagnation
E219. Liver - Moisture heat in liver and gall bladder
E220. Liver - Fire
E221. Liver - Gall bladder Qi-Empty
E222. Liver - Cold in the liver meridian
E223. Liver - Qi stagnation
E224. Liver - Wind
E225. Liver - Wind with ascending liver Yang
E226. Liver - Wind with blood anemic
E227. Liver - Wind with extreme heat
E228. Lung - Qi deficiency
E229. Lung - Mucus-moisture in the lungs
E230. Lung - Mucus-heat in the lungs
E231. Lung - Mucus-cold in the lungs
E232. Lung - Dryness of the lungs
E233. Lung - Wind-heat attacks the lungs
E234. Lung - Wind-cold affects the lungs
E235. Lung - Yin deficiency
E236. Stomach - Bloodstagnation
E237. Stomach - Fire
E238. Stomach - Cold with liquid
E239. Stomach - Nutrition stagnation
E240. Stomach - Qi deficiency
E241. Stomach - Rebellious Qi
E242. Stomach - Yin Emptiness
E243. Spleen - Heat and moisture attack the spleen
E244. Spleen - Coldness and moisture affects the spleen
E245. Spleen - Qi deficiency
E246. Spleen - Qi deficiency + Declining spleen Qi
E247. Spleen - Qi deficiency + spleen does not control the blood
E248. Spleen - Yang deficiency
E249. Kidney - Heart and kidney no longer communicate
E250. Kidney - Jing deficiency
E251. Kidney - Kidneys cannot receive the Qi
E252. Kidney - Qi is not stable
E253. Kidney - Yang deficiency
E254. Kidney - Yin deficiency

For further information visit di-book.com.